A TIBETAN FAMILY

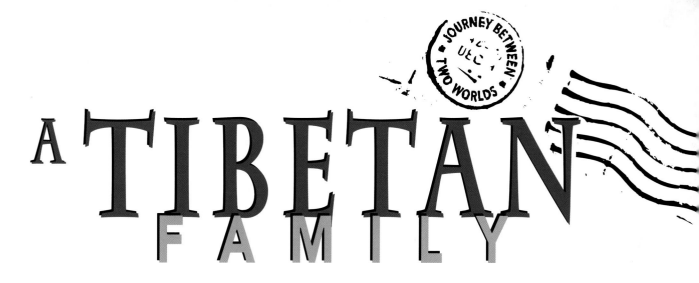

A TIBETAN FAMILY

By Stephen Chicoine

Lerner Publications Company • Minneapolis

Website address: www.lernerbooks.com

A pronunciation guide can be found on page 54.

The interviews for this book were conducted in 1996 and in 1997.

LIBRARY OF CONGRESS CATALOGING-IN-PUBLICATION DATA

Chicoine, Stephen
    A Tibetan family / by Stephen Chicoine.
      p. cm. — (Journey between two worlds)
    Includes index.
    Summary: Presents an overview of Tibetan history before relating the story of a refugee family who fled their homeland in 1959 and eventually moved to Columbus, Ohio, where they became American citizens.
    ISBN 0-8225-3408-8 (lib. bdg. : alk. paper)
    1. Tibetan American families—Ohio—Columbus—Juvenile literature.
    2. Refugees, Political—Ohio—Columbus—Juvenile literature.
    3. Refugees, Political—China—Tibet—Juvenile literature.
    4. Tibetan Americans—Ohio—Columbus—Social life and customs—Juvenile literature. 5. Columbus (Ohio)—Social life and customs—Juvenile literature. [1. Tibetan Americans. 2. Refugees. 3. Columbus (Ohio)—Social life and customs.] I. Title. II. Series.
F499.C79T534 1998
306.85′0977′57—DC21   97-12645

Manufactured in the United States of America
1 2 3 4 5 6 – SP – 03 02 01 00 99 98

AUTHOR'S NOTE

In 1987 I spent a month traveling across Tibet. One can never be the same after such an unforgettable experience. The land, the people, and the culture make Tibet a truly special place for any traveler. What I saw and felt in Tibet caused me to want to become involved with refugees and in the struggle for human rights in some small way. I believe that it is possible for those of us outside Tibet to learn from the gentle Tibetan people, with their contagious smiles and peaceful ways, the respect they show all living things, and their wonderful sense of compassion and understanding. This has been their gift to me over the years.

I wish to thank the Tsewang family—Tsewang, Jampa, Passang, and Tenzin—for the warm hospitality they extended to me, and especially for their never-ending enthusiasm in supporting my effort to tell a small piece of the Tibetan refugee story. Rinchen Dharlo of The Tibet Fund introduced me to this truly remarkable couple and their children. My friends Professor Anne Klein of Rice University in Houston, Texas, and Joshua Cutler of the Tibetan Buddhist Learning Center in Washington, New Jersey, offered advice on matters concerning Tibetan Buddhism. Bhuchung Tsering provided assistance on refugee matters. Dr. Paul Zanowiak was kind enough to let me photograph items from his collection of Tibetan rugs. Most importantly, I acknowledge my wife, Mary Ann, whose patience and understanding allowed me the time to work on such a satisfying and worthwhile project.

This Tibetan refugee works as a weaver in Kalimpong, India. After the Chinese takeover of Tibet in 1949, many Tibetans fled their homeland and ended up in India and Nepal, both of which lie south of Tibet.

SERIES INTRODUCTION

 What they have left behind is sometimes a living nightmare of war and hunger that most Americans can hardly begin to imagine. As refugees set out to start a new life in another country, they are torn by many feelings. They may wish they didn't have to leave their homeland. They may fear giving up the only life they have ever known. Many may also feel excitement and hope as they struggle to build a better life in a new country.

People who move from one place to another are called migrants. Two types of migrants are immigrants and refugees. Immigrants choose to leave their homelands, usually to improve their standards of living. They may be leaving behind poverty, famine (hunger), or a failing economy. They may be pursuing a better job or reuniting with family members.

Refugees, on the other hand, often have no choice but to flee their homeland to protect their own personal safety. How could anyone be in so much danger?

The red flag (above) of the People's Republic of China (PRC) flies in front of Potala Palace in Lhasa, the capital of Tibet. A Tibetan Buddhist monk (left) fingers his prayer beads. Beginning in 1949, the PRC persecuted Tibetan monks and destroyed many religious sites.

The government of his or her country is either unable or unwilling to protect its citizens from persecution, or cruel treatment. In many cases, the government is actually the cause of the persecution. Government leaders or another group within the country may be persecuting anyone of a certain race, religion, or ethnic background. Or they may persecute those who belong to a particular social group or who hold political opinions that are not accepted by the government.

From the 1950s through the mid-1970s, the number of refugees worldwide held steady at between 1.5 and 2.5 million. The number began to rise sharply in 1976. By the mid-1990s, it approached 20 million. These figures do not include people who are fleeing disasters

Although many thousands of Tibetans have fled their homeland since the 1950s, only 3,000 have come to the United States. This group from New Mexico traveled to Houston, Texas, in 1995 to see the Dalai Lama, the spiritual leader of the Tibetan people.

such as famine (estimated to be at least 10 million). Nor do they include those who are forced to leave their homes but stay within their own countries (about 27 million).

As this rise in refugees and other migrants continues, countries that have long welcomed newcomers are beginning to close their doors. Some U.S. citizens question whether the United States should accept refugees when it cannot even meet the needs of all its own people. On the other hand, experts point out that the number of refugees is small—less than 20 percent of all migrants worldwide—so refugees really don't have a very big impact on the nation. Still others suggest that the tide of refugees could be slowed through greater efforts to address the problems that force people to flee. There are no easy answers in this ongoing debate.

This book is one in a series called *Journey Between Two Worlds*, which looks at the lives of refugee families—their difficulties and triumphs. Each book describes the journey of a family from their homeland to the United States and how they adjust to a new life in America while still preserving traditions from their homeland. The series makes no attempt to join the debate about refugees. Instead, *Journey Between Two Worlds* hopes to give readers a better understanding of the daily struggles and joys of a refugee family.

In 1987 Tibetan refugees protested in India against the killing of eight Tibetans in Lhasa. The deaths took place when Chinese security forces broke up demonstrations demanding greater freedoms for Tibetans.

There is no eye like understanding,
No blindness like ignorance.

(From *Tibetan Folk Tales* by Fredrick and Audrey Hyde-Chambers. Boulder, CO: Shambhala, 1981.)

 Twelve-year-old Tenzin Tsewang vividly remembers her first day of school in the United States. "I was in first grade. I was new. People in my class didn't know me. They started calling me Chinese. I got really mad. I talked to the teacher and then to the principal. I said, 'They're calling me Chinese. I'm not Chinese. I'm from Tibet.'"

Tenzin's teacher called Tenzin's parents. She asked Tsewang and Jampa, Tenzin's father and mother, to speak to the school about Tibet. Jampa and Tenzin prepared Tibetan food for Tenzin's class, with the help of her father and her 15-year-old brother, Passang. The family also gave a presentation in front of 500 students at Tenzin's school, which is located in the Tsewangs' hometown of Columbus, Ohio. Ever since that day, Tenzin's classmates have appreciated what it means to be Tibetan.

Located in central Asia, Tibet is a vast land about the size of the state of Alaska. China surrounds Tibet on three sides, while India, Nepal, Bhutan, and Myanmar (Burma) lie along Tibet's southern border. People often call Tibet the Roof of the World because it lies so high above sea level and is surrounded by massive mountain ranges. These ranges include the Kunlun to the north, the Daxue to the east, the Karakoram to the west, and the Himalaya to the south. The Himalaya Mountains contain 30 peaks with elevations reaching more than 24,000 feet above sea level. The most famous is Mount Everest (29,028 feet), the highest place on earth.

Yaks (left), a type of wild ox, are ideal beasts of burden in Tibet. They provide herders with milk, meat, and hides. Tibet has a dry, cold climate, mostly because the Himalaya Mountains (above) prevent rains from reaching Tibet's elevated grasslands.

Tsewang (right), *Tenzin's father, received a special blessing from the Dalai Lama during the leader's visit to the United States in the early 1990s.*

The Tibetan region is home to 6 million people. They speak the Tibetan language. But since 1949, when China invaded Tibet, Mandarin Chinese has been the imposed official language. Most Tibetans live in cities and farming communities in southern Tibet, where crops flourish in the area's fertile river valleys. Some families migrate (move) every year across the Chang-Tang, a vast plateau (highland) covering northern and central Tibet. These nomadic families herd sheep and yaks, taking the animals from one grassy pasture to another according to the season.

Tibetans are a deeply spiritual people. They have a long history of practicing the religion of Buddhism, which was founded in the 500s B.C. by an Indian philosopher and teacher named Siddhartha Gautama. The leader of the Tibetan people is His Holiness, the Dalai Lama, Tibet's most important religious figure.

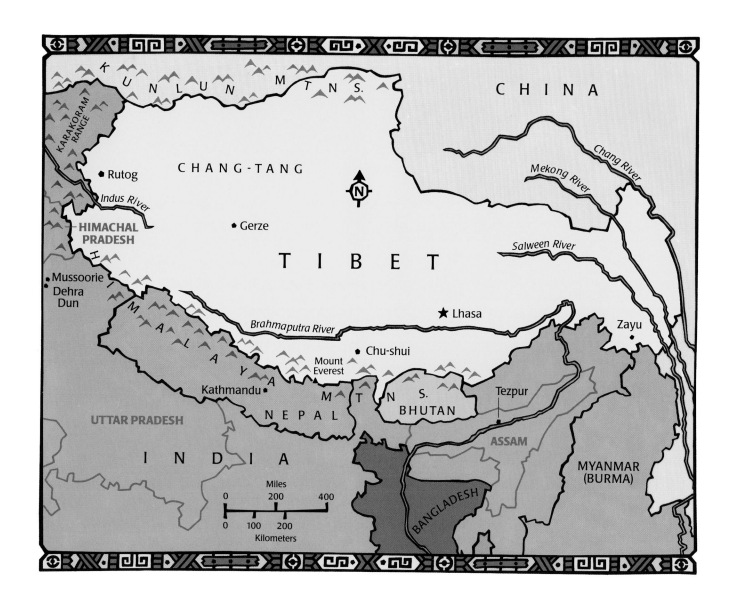

 Indian Buddhists introduced Buddhism to Tibet in the A.D. 600s during the reign of the Tibetan leader Songtsen Gampo. He built a powerful empire in central Asia. The empire was strong enough to battle the Chinese for control of profitable trade routes linking the Far East to Europe.

In 779 two famous Indian Buddhist teachers, Santarakshita and Padmasambhava, founded Tibet's first university. The school hosted a major religious debate in 792 to determine whether Tibetans would follow Indian or Chinese Buddhist teachings. Indian Buddhism emphasizes that spiritual enlightenment is achieved only through dedicated effort and practice over a series of incarnations, or life cycles. Chinese Buddhists, on the other hand, believe that enlightenment can be attained right away. The Indian teachings prevailed at the debate, and the Chinese Buddhist teachers were expelled from Tibet.

A Tibetan thangka *(religious painting on cloth) shows scenes from the life of the Buddha. Buddhists view the Buddha as a unique person who discovered the path to salvation and shared it with others.*

The Mongol commander Genghis Khan took over all of central Asia, including Tibet, in the 1200s.

The image of Tsong Khapa, founder of the Yellow Hat sect of Tibetan Buddhism, is the central focus of a huge carpet stretched on a Tibetan hillside during an annual religious gathering.

In the 1200s, a mighty conqueror named Genghis Khan united the Mongols—a group of nomadic peoples from the northern part of central Asia. The Mongols eventually conquered most of Asia and even threatened Europe. In 1240 the Mongols became the first foreign power to invade Tibet. Because of the invasion, Mongols were exposed to Tibetan Buddhism. In time, many Mongols converted to the religion.

Genghis Khan's grandson, Kublai Khan, became the leader of the Mongols in 1260. He became a powerful supporter of Buddhism. When the Mongols conquered China in 1279, they brought their Tibetan spiritual leaders with them. Although the Chinese drove out the Mongols about 100 years later, the Mongols maintained their spiritual ties to Tibet.

In the 1300s, a Tibetan religious leader named Tsong Khapa founded the Gelukpa sect, or the Yellow Hat sect of Tibetan Buddhism. In 1578 Sonam Gyatso, an important Gelukpa abbott (head of a monastery), traveled to Mongolia and converted the leading Mongol prince and his followers to the Gelukpa sect. The prince gave Sonam Gyatso the formal title Dalai Lama, meaning roughly "Ocean of Wisdom." The Gelukpas' connection to the powerful Mongols allowed the Yellow Hats to gain control of all of Tibet. As a result, a succession of dalai lamas ruled Tibet for several hundred years.

Lobsang Gyatso, the fifth Dalai Lama (1617–1682), unified Tibet politically for the first time. Under his rule, many structures were built throughout Tibet, including Potala Palace (above), which he made his winter residence.

After the PRC took over Tibet, Chinese soldiers, as well as ethnic Chinese civilians, arrived in large numbers to settle there.

In 1910 a Chinese army invaded Tibet. The Dalai Lama fled to India, where he developed strong ties during two years of exile. Revolution in China in 1911 brought down the ruling Chinese dynasty (governing family), and Chinese soldiers were forced to withdraw from Tibet. With the Dalai Lama's return the next year, Tibet was ruled once again by its own people.

After almost 40 years of civil war, Communists gained control of China in 1949, established the People's Republic of China (PRC), and invaded Tibet. Tibet's small army was no match for the large, well-equipped army of the PRC, which quickly overpowered the Tibetans. To merge Tibet into the new Chinese Communist regime, the Chinese began an effort to erase Tibetans' identity as a separate people within a distinct nation. The Chinese tried to do this by attacking Tibetan Buddhism, which is at the heart of Tibetan culture. Chinese soldiers looted and destroyed monasteries. They also imprisoned or killed many monks and lamas. They ordered Tibetans to give up their religion, beating and imprisoning those who refused. In addition, the PRC started an ongoing program to resettle large numbers of Chinese people in Tibet, where they wanted to firmly establish Chinese culture.

Ganden Monastery in the Lhasa River Valley has seen better days. The PRC damaged many religious buildings and killed thousands of Buddhist monks as part of an ongoing effort to destroy Tibetans' identity as a separate people.

By 1959 Tibetan resistance groups had delivered several serious blows to the Chinese occupation forces. At this time, the Chinese were pressing the Dalai Lama to visit China, and many Tibetans believed that the Chinese planned to kidnap or even to kill their leader. Concerns grew until March 1959, when tens of thousands of Tibetans rushed to Norbulingka Palace and to

On March 10, 1959, crowds of Tibetan women gathered outside Potala Palace (left), as well as outside of Norbulingka Palace, to protest the Chinese occupation.

Many feared for the safety of the Dalai Lama, who left Tibet in secret on March 17, 1959. After nearly a month of grueling travel, the Dalai Lama (left, wearing glasses) *arrived in India. He eventually set up a government-in-exile (a government outside the country) in Dharmsala, a town in northern India.*

Potala Palace in Tibet's capital city of Lhasa, where the Dalai Lama lived. They came to protect their leader and to protest the Chinese occupation of Tibet. As the days passed, the situation between Chinese troops and Tibetan protesters became increasingly tense. The Dalai Lama tried unsuccessfully to negotiate peace with the Chinese. The protesters and the troops clashed, leaving thousands of people dead. Chinese soldiers arrested thousands more, quickly squelching the uprising. The Dalai Lama fled into exile in India. From there he decided he could best help his people by telling the world what was happening in Tibet.

Since the 1950s, the Chinese have killed the majority of Tibet's 4,000 holiest, highest-ranking lamas. Only a few thousand of Tibet's 600,000 monks have been able to escape to neighboring India. Those who remained in Tibet have suffered imprisonment and torture. Besides religious leaders, nearly 1 million Tibetans have lost their lives under Chinese rule.

From his residence in exile, the Dalai Lama has acknowledged that the Chinese Communists may be too powerful to drive out of Tibet. Since 1988 he has been urging the PRC to consider a plan by which Chinese-occupied Tibet would become a zone of peace. The

(Above) *A poster urges Americans to stop buying Chinese goods as a way to demonstrate support for Tibet.* (Right) *The Dalai Lama travels throughout the world, speaking about his homeland. He has put together a five-point plan that he hopes will result in a peaceful resolution to China's occupation of Tibet.*

Tibetans ask not for political independence but for a self-governing, democratic state within the PRC. They ask for respect for human rights, a stop to the dumping of nuclear waste in Tibet, and an end to the massive transfer of Chinese into Tibet. Tibetans wish to save their people and to preserve their culture in their native land.

 At the time of the 1959 uprising, Tenzin's father, Tsewang, was a 15-year-old monk at Takhupai Monastery near the town of Chushui, located outside Lhasa. Tsewang's oldest brother, Kapchu-la, was *kenpo* (head abbot) of the monastery, where two other brothers were also monks. With their lives in danger, Tsewang and a group of fellow monks fled their homeland. Tsewang's brothers at Takhupai remained behind. Like many groups of Tibetan refugees, Tsewang and his companions traveled day and night, heading across the treacherous Himalaya Mountains to safety in India. Often they were just ahead of Chinese soldiers.

Near the Indian border, Tibetan refugees cross a treacherous gorge by using logs as a bridge.

Tsewang remembers, "I left Tibet very sadly and suddenly with my horse and my fellow monks. My heart was beating very strongly for my parents, brothers and sisters, and everything I left behind. My horse became very weak and the look in his eyes made me feel even more sad. I quietly sobbed with my horse, which I loved so much. He was too weak to continue, and I had to leave him in a grassy meadow. It was very hard for me."

Like thousands of other fleeing Tibetans, Tsewang made his way to the Indian border. From there he continued on foot to a large Tibetan refugee camp near Tezpur, in northeastern India.

Lobsang (another of Tsewang's brothers) later arrived at this same town with a group of Tibetan monks. The group's border crossing into India had been very dangerous, and Lobsang's clothing was torn with bullet holes. Tsewang is certain his brother and the other monks survived because of their *tung-wa* (religious thread cords believed to protect those who wear them). Although he was relieved to see his brother, Tsewang doesn't recall feeling joyful at the time. "I felt deep sadness. We had lost our country. Country is very important. So always inside, we are sad."

The two brothers eventually were sent to work building roads in the Chamba District of Himachal Pradesh, an Indian state bordering Tibet. Tsewang remembers the dangerous work. "Rocks would sometimes fall and crush people. Some people would fall down the mountainside. So many people died."

After the first year of roadwork, Tsewang began suffering from severe headaches, and his eyesight began to fail. He says, "My eyesight became bad and then worse and worse. Each month it was like a flashlight [that fades over time]." The Tsewangs still don't know what caused the problem. Jampa says, "A couple of his friends had the same problems, too."

After Tsewang and his brother Lobsang arrived in India, they worked on a construction crew that was building roads through the Himalaya Mountains. During this time, Tsewang lost his sight.

25

Lobsang took Tsewang to see different doctors about his eyes. But nothing helped, and the problem only worsened. Tsewang refused to give up. He enrolled in a school for the blind in Dehra Dun, a town in the neighboring state of Uttar Pradesh, India. In Dehra Dun, Tsewang also took lessons in English and Hindi (one of India's official languages). Later he learned to read both languages in Braille, a system of writing for the blind.

In 1965, after three years at the school in Dehra Dun, Tsewang moved to nearby Mussoorie, where he joined the Tibetan Homes Foundation as a handicraft instructor. He served in this position for nearly 25 years and became well known among Tibetans living in exile. Mrs. Taring, the foundation's general secretary, became like a mother to Tsewang. She saw to it that Tsewang and others were able to greet the Dalai Lama for a personal blessing each time the leader visited Mussoorie.

After taking courses in a school for the blind, Tsewang became a teacher. He showed young students how to make Tibetan handicrafts (top). *Tsewang* (third from left) *also occasionally joined other Tibetans to perform Tibetan dances* (left).

Tenzin's mother, Jampa, was born to a nomadic family who raised horses, ponies, yaks, sheeps, and goats in the Chang-Tang region of northern Tibet. From her distant memory, Jampa remembers only "the open land of green grass with thousands of animals and countless beautiful flowers everywhere." Jampa's family fled Tibet in 1959 when she was just a small child. She recalls the trek across the Himalaya Mountains. "I came along with my parents by foot all the way from Tibet to Kathmandu [the capital of Nepal]. One day I fell down and almost went down the mountainside into the river far below. My mother caught me."

Not all of the family made the difficult passage to Nepal safely. Jampa's eight-year-old sister, Bhuti, became sick and died. Her baby brother, Tsering, also became very ill. The family is grateful for the powers of a religious man, whom they credit with restoring young Tsering to life.

The family lived in Kathmandu until 1964, when they received permission from the Indian government to join other Tibetan refugees in nothern India. Jampa's parents were then sent with the other adults to work on road construction in Himachal Pradesh. Jampa and her younger brothers and sisters were placed in various schools for refugee children. Jampa and one sister were placed in Kangra School. Six months later, they

Jampa went to see the Taj Mahal, a famous tomb in northern India, in 1977. The next year, Tsewang and Jampa married in Mussoorie.

were sent to live at the Tibetan Homes Foundation in Mussoorie. Their parents worked in a region that took several days to reach from Mussoorie.

"We missed each other a lot," Jampa says. "Somehow our parents kept in touch with us whenever they could. They had a very tough time with the road construction, with their children being far away from them and in different places, and with losing our motherland to the Chinese."

Tsewang and Jampa eventually met in Mussoorie, where they married in 1978. Several hundred people attended the three-day wedding. Afterward the couple lived apart for almost a year. Jampa worked in New Delhi, the capital of India, before finding a job with the Central School for Tibetans in Mussoorie.

Even though Tsewang and Jampa were happy together, they worried and wondered about family and friends they had left behind in Tibet. Getting information about Tibet was almost impossible at that time. China did not allow people outside the region to travel to or communicate with Tibet. One night in 1978, Tsewang and Jampa were returning from friends' weddings. Tsewang was overcome with sorrow and began to cry. He explains, "Both of the friends getting married had such nice parents. And I had very, very strong feelings. I felt that something had happened to my parents."

A TIBETAN WEDDING

Tsewang and Jampa's wedding in India lasted three days. Traditional Tibetan celebrations can last up to two weeks. On the first day, the couple finalized preparations for the ceremony, which was to take place on the second day. Friends and guests who had come from out of town for the wedding spent time socializing. Some friends came from as far away as Great Britain and the United States.

On the second day, Tsewang and Jampa went early in the morning to the local temple to make offerings and to be married. The Tarings, Jampa's mother, and Jampa's brother accompanied them. From the temple, Tsewang and Jampa went to their home. They prepared to meet their guests in the main room with Jampa's mother. She made an offering to the family's altar. Before any of the guests filed in, the three of them each

placed a *kata* (a Tibetan silk scarf symbolizing respect) around a framed photo of the Dalai Lama.

Then the couple and Jampa's mother sat on the carpet to await their guests, each of whom hung a kata around the Dalai Lama's portrait. The guests also placed katas on Tsewang, Jampa, and Jampa's mother. Several times they had to remove the katas to make room for more. People also presented the newlyweds with gifts. After the guests shared tea and raisin rice with the couple for good luck, festivities began. Jampa explains, "There was lots of dancing and eating, all day."

The third day of the wedding was a giant thank-you party for all the people who had helped to shop and to prepare food. Jampa shakes her head and says, "No one would accept our money for any of this."

During his 1981 visit to Tibet, Tsewang and his sister posed in front of Potala Palace. Before leaving India, Tsewang traveled to Dharmsala to seek the Dalai Lama's blessing. The Dalai Lama asked Tsewang to tell his family and friends that Tibetans in exile were making efforts to safeguard Tibetan culture.

By 1980 the Communist leadership in Tibet had changed, and the Chinese were beginning to allow people from outside Tibet to visit and communicate with the region. So Tsewang wrote a letter to his parents. He says, "We had no idea what their address was. We had no idea whether they were there or not. We just sent a letter with their name to where they had been so many years before." After many months, a letter arrived for Tsewang from Tibet. It was the first he had heard from his family in 21 years.

From the letter, Tsewang learned that his father had died in 1978. In fact, his father had died at the time of the weddings when Tsewang had felt so much grief. But Tsewang's mother was still alive. For so long, Tsewang had feared that both his parents were dead. Reading the letter "was like she was back from the dead," Tsewang says.

Tsewang applied to the Chinese government for permission to visit Tibet. He was granted a visa and was among the first refugees to return to Tibet.

Tsewang returned to his homeland in 1981. At the border, a Tibetan government official agreed to drive Tsewang to his family home. The official knocked on the door and said, "Your son from India, I have brought him here." Tsewang embraced his mother. He explored her hands with his own. He recalls, "When I felt her hand, it was broken here and there from many

(Right) *Tsewang* (holding puppy) *and his family members surround his mother* (seated). (Below) *Lobsang, who had emigrated to Columbus, Ohio, also visited Tibet at this time.*

years of hard work. For a couple of hours, we couldn't talk. We just cried and touched each other."

Tsewang weeps as he tells of his reunion with his family and friends. "I told my story. They told their stories. We sat on the floor and talked until early morning." The family talked a lot about their father. And Tsewang heard news of Kapchu-la, the brother who had been a kenpo at Takhupai Monastery. Kapchu-la had suffered greatly from many nights of public beatings and humiliations. Long after the Chinese had destroyed the monastery, he continued to go to the site of the ancient holy place to pray.

Tsewang spent two and a half months in Tibet. While he was there, he bought kitchen utensils for his family, who could afford to purchase very little. And he gave money to whitewash (paint) the family home.

Tsewang's brother Lobsang, who had emigrated by this time to the United States, had received permission to visit Tibet during Tsewang's visit. The family wanted to greet him with a clean and freshly painted house. Tsewang explains, "When Tibet was free, everyone whitewashed before the Tibetan New Year. It isn't done anymore because people have a hard time just to get food. Everyone is pretty poor. [Painting the house] was special because our brother was coming from the United States."

After Lobsang's arrival, the family went on a pilgrimage (sacred journey) to the monasteries at Lhasa. Most of them were in ruins. Tsewang says, "I prayed at all the monasteries. I prayed from my heart for all those who died for our country."

Jampa holds Tenzin as she celebrates her first birthday.

 The year after Tsewang's visit to Tibet, Passang was born. Tenzin was born three years later in 1985. The children enjoyed life in Mussoorie. They had good friends and good teachers. But opportunities in India were limited, and the Tsewangs had hoped for some time to move to the United States. Jampa says, "We wanted to go to the United States to be reunited with Lobsang and in the hopes of a better education for our kids."

As a U.S. citizen, Lobsang had the right to apply to the U.S. government to bring family members to the United States. From his home in Columbus, Ohio, Lobsang had begun the application process in 1978. But it was many years before the application was approved. In the meantime, Lobsang and his wife, Chemi, enlisted the aid of their American friends John and Bess Devol to sponsor the Tsewangs. As sponsors the Devols agreed to pay the family's airfare and to help them settle into their new life in Columbus.

Finally in 1989, the Tsewang family received permission to go to the United States. Tsewang and Jampa attended many farewell parties before leaving India, where they had made their home for so many years and had earned the respect of their community. Jampa says, "When we left, our friends and coworkers came to say good-bye to us. They gave us katas. Our necks were piled with katas. It was really something to remember, really remarkable. We were crying."

The Tsewang family flew to New York from New Delhi. Although Tenzin was only four years old at the time, she remembers some of the trip. "It was the first time we ever flew. It was kind of scary for me because there were hardly any Tibetans. My first English words were 'excuse me' because that was what I kept hearing on the plane. Then I got lost in the airport in New York. I was scared, but they finally found me."

When Tenzin was about four, she and her family—including her older brother Passang—followed Uncle Lobsang to the United States. Before they left, they traveled to Dharmsala to say good-bye to the Dalai Lama and to receive his blessing.

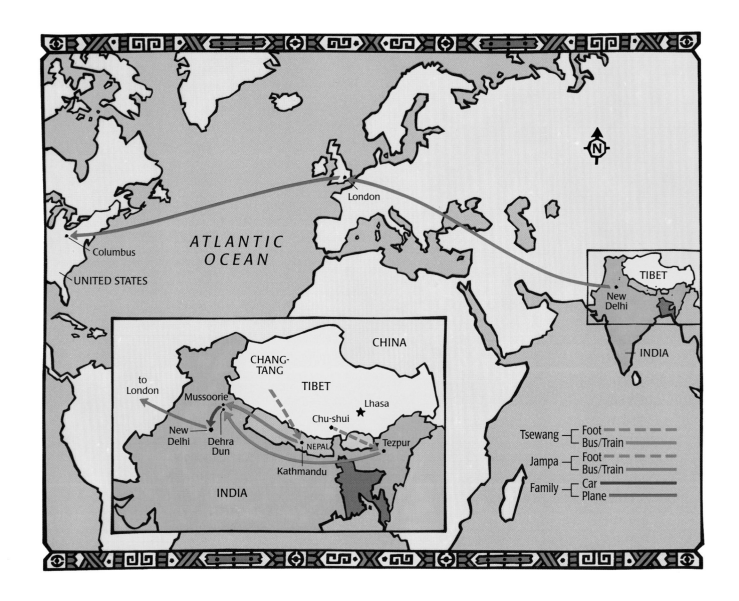

Passang, who was seven when the family left India, recalls arriving in Columbus. "It was strange. There were a lot of people, and we had to find my aunt and uncle [in the crowd]." Jampa adds, "Lobsang and Chemi met us with American flags, and we offered them katas."

At first Tsewang and his family lived with Lobsang and Chemi. Soon Tsewang and Jampa had jobs and had saved enough money to move into their own apartment. Even before the family had arrived in Ohio, Lobsang had researched jobs for his brother. He helped Tsewang find work at a company that hires people to perform jobs they can do by touch. Such tasks include strapping bundles of unfolded boxes and slipping O-rings onto small fittings. Tsewang is one of the company's best workers. His supervisor says, "I can put Tsewang in the back warehouse and never have to check on him. He can do the work of two."

Jampa found a job working nights as a cashier at a 24-hour convenience store. Because the family didn't own a car, Jampa often walked to and from her job—a 20-minute trip each way. When he could, Lobsang would pick up Jampa when her shift ended at midnight.

(Facing page) *Tsewang fled Tibet at 15, traveling day and night to reach India. Jampa escaped when she was a toddler. She and her family tramped across the Himalaya Mountains to Nepal. The Tsewangs eventually made their way to Columbus* (above), *the capital of Ohio.*

Tsewang (above) *and Jampa* (right) *both have full-time jobs.*

As Jampa was walking home late one night, Pastor David Brown and his wife, Carla, saw Jampa and worried about her safety. They stopped to offer her a ride home. Jampa accepted, and the two families became friends. Pastor Brown says, "Jampa is one of the nicest people you'd ever want to know. She'd give you the shirt off her back and her last dollar."

Jampa soon decided she needed to learn to drive for herself. She says, "In America you have to be able to learn to use a car." Driving was a challenge for Jampa, the daughter of a nomadic family. She says, "I had never even touched a bicycle!"

By this time, Jampa had quit her job at the convenience store and had two new jobs. Her workday started at 9:00 A.M. at a steak house, where she managed a salad bar. When her shift was over in mid-afternoon, she rushed to her second job at a giant 24-hour superstore. At this combination grocery and department store, Jampa worked as a cashier until 3:00 A.M.

To learn to drive, Jampa wanted someone with patience who could work around her tight schedule. Friends introduced Jampa to a couple of their friends, who volunteered to teach Jampa to drive on her days off. Jampa says, "Phyllis and Nuanna were great. They used their time, their car, their gas." Jampa passed her driver's test on the second try, and the Tsewangs bought a used car.

Passang is eager to get his license and drive. He likes reading car and truck magazines. "I like the trucks with the sides almost touching the ground, with the small wheels and special paint jobs," he says. In the meantime, Passang is the navigator when Jampa drives. Tsewang laughs and says, "Passang, he knows all the roads." But Passang is interested in cars for other reasons. He's fascinated by mechanical things and wants to study engineering when he goes to college.

These days Jampa no longer works two jobs. She is employed full-time at the superstore, which sits at the

Despite lack of experience, Jampa was determined to learn to drive and passed her driver's test on the second try—the cause of great celebration among the family.

edge of a giant parking lot near the family's apartment. She has been with the store long enough to proudly wear a service award on a chain around her neck. Nearly all of Jampa's coworkers know she is Tibetan. She has a pleasant smile for everyone, and some of her customers have also come to know her story. Jampa laughs as she explains how regular customers sometimes say, "Well, here we go again through the checkout line with the Tibetan lady."

As far as the Tsewangs know, they and Lobsang's family are the only Tibetans in Columbus. Without fellow Tibetans to rely on, Tsewang and Jampa have had difficulty adjusting to some of the social aspects of life in the United States. Jampa explains, "We were very social with our friends in India. Here people are good, nice, friendly. But they don't know us. We don't know them. No one has time to share with each other. Everybody has to rush to their jobs. So our main problem here was loneliness."

Tenzin helps her mother through some of the lonely times.

She continues, "In India, when you offer to help someone, they thank you. They do not suspect anything. Here, when you try to be helpful, sometimes people think, Who are you? What are you trying to do? I don't need your help. It's hard to get used to. We were so homesick for almost two years that we nearly went back to India."

Despite the loneliness, the Tsewangs are thankful for the refuge the United States has provided. Tsewang says, "The main thing is that America is a free country. If we follow the laws, then nothing is wrong, everything is fine. This is a good country."

 The beginning of a new life in the United States was much easier for Tenzin and Passang than it was for their parents. Passang had already learned to read and write English in the Tibetan schools in India. He easily settled into school in Columbus. "When I came here, they said my handwriting was good, so they put me in second grade," he says.

Passang made friends through sports activities. In India he had played basketball and rooted for a local team. He remembers, "We had our own basketball team. Their arena was right beside our home. We used to go to watch them." In the United States, Passang

A big basketball fan, Passang shows his support for the Charlotte Hornets, North Carolina's National Basketball Association team.

With the Tibetan flag as a backdrop, Tenzin makes a presentation to some of her classmates.

wears Air Jordans—basketball shoes endorsed by star player Michael Jordan. Passang also follows the National Basketball Association (NBA) season on television and dreams of going to an NBA game someday.

Because Tenzin was too young for school when the family arrived in Ohio, she learned English in other ways. Jampa laughs and says, "She learned English by herself. I didn't teach her much. [She learned] from TV and the neighborhood children."

Tenzin and her brother have spoken English with one another from the time they first came to Columbus. When Tenzin started school, her English improved greatly. Both children are now completely fluent in English as well as in Tibetan, which they continue to speak with their family. Neither Tenzin nor Passang has the slightest accent when speaking English. Their parents' accents, on the other hand, indicate they were born abroad.

Mornings begin at the Tsewang home with a mixture of Tibetan and American rituals. Tenzin gets up at 5:00 A.M. and watches cartoons while she eats her breakfast. Her father listens to tape recordings of a lama reciting prayers and then catches a special city bus that takes him directly to work. At 7:00 A.M., Tenzin catches her bus to a Columbus middle school where she attends sixth grade in an accelerated program for gifted students.

Tenzin has only good things to say about school. "It's great!" She loves to read, especially the scary *Goosebumps* series. She's read the autobiography of the Dalai Lama and plans to read more about Tibet.

Tsewang is very proud of his daughter. Tenzin is consistently on her school's super honor roll. Her father says, "Tenzin's classmates call her with math questions. She helps them." Last year her class performed *Macbeth,* a play by William Shakespeare. Tenzin had the starring role of Lady Macbeth and enjoyed the experience, especially the costumes. She was challenged playing the role of her character, whom she describes as "cruel and deceiving because she wanted power."

In addition to her achievements in the classroom, Tenzin has also developed good relationships with her teachers. A letter to Tenzin from one of her teachers reads, "You may not know it, but you and your family have taught me a lot this year. You and your family are special people. I hope you try to follow the example that your parents set for you."

Every evening Tenzin and Passang do their homework. They also do chores their parents have assigned to them. Both children help cook and clean up. Tsewang smiles and says, "When everyone works together, then everyone is happy." After each of his bits of wisdom, Tsewang gives a little laugh.

Passang (above) *helps out in the kitchen, while Tenzin* (below) *works at the computer.*

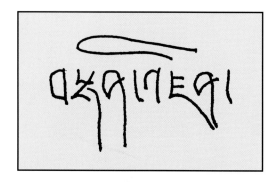

Preserving Tibetan culture is very important to the Tsewangs. (Above) *Both Tenzin and Passang work at reading and writing the Tibetan language.* (Top) *Tenzin practices by writing her name in Tibetan.*

Jampa says, "In our country, we teach the kids from the beginning to cook, to wash, to be prepared for their life." With some families [in the United States], there's not enough love from the heart. Parents give their kids things, but that's not enough."

After schoolwork and household chores are done, Tenzin and Passang study Tibetan culture. Tenzin says, "I practice prayers from a Tibetan prayer book." Tsewang remarks, "She studies very hard. She reads sometimes until 10:30 at night, almost 11:00."

Because Jampa works at night during the week, she isn't always available to help Tenzin and Passang learn to read and write in their native Tibetan language. As a solution, Jampa records Tibetan texts onto cassette tapes so Tsewang can work with the children. Tenzin and Passang read from the many different texts. Tsewang doesn't know all the material by heart, but with Jampa's tapes, he can follow along and help the children with their pronunciation. Whenever they have time, Tenzin and Passang practice writing Tibetan script by copying from books printed in India. In the hallway, the family has put up printed sheets that list the gods of Tibetan Buddhism and the meaning of the elements of the Tibetan national flag.

Tsewang and Jampa have a clear understanding of the importance of education. "Education is in our hands. It can never be taken away from you. It is with you until you die." Tsewang chuckles, "I don't want my children to be donkeyheads and not know anything about our culture." He gestures with his arms and adds, "You know, donkeys have heads this big, but they still don't know anything. You hold something up to a donkey's face, and they don't know what it is." Tsewang laughs again. He enjoys laughing, but he is very serious about his children's education. He adds, "[Teaching our children about Tibet] is very important. If we do not teach them, then they will forget. After we die, they must teach their own children."

 Anyone entering the Tsewangs' home might feel as if they were in Tibet. A *dha-nyen* (Tibetan guitar) hangs on the wall over the kitchen table. A *shambu* (cloth) covers the top of the doorway leading from the kitchen to the living quarters. (In a Tibetan monastery, the shambu cloth traditionally covers the outside door.) On one wall of the living room is a giant watercolor of the Potala Palace, the former winter residence of the Dalai Lama. Another wall is lined with Tibetan *thangkas*— elaborate, religious paintings on cotton or linen bordered with silk. Painted by Tibetan monks, each thangka has a main image of an important Tibetan

A richly colored thangka hangs on a wall of the Tsewangs' living room. Each thangka holds the image of a Buddhist religious figure.

A SPECIAL THANGKA

One of the Tsewang family's thangkas comes from an ancient Tibetan monastery near the one in which Tsewang once lived. The image on this thangka is of Chenrezi, a Buddhist god of compassion and mercy. During Tsewang's trip to Tibet in 1981, an older monk gave the thangka to him. The Chinese had imprisoned this monk for 20 years. To hide the thangka, he had rolled it up and tucked it into his robe. At night he had used it as a pillow.

Buddhist figure. Tibetans use thangkas as aids for prayer and meditation.

Like most Tibetan families, the Tsewangs have a traditional Buddhist altar in their home. The altar contains small bronze statues of various Tibetan Buddhist religious figures. Tibetans pray to these beings in the hopes of enriching their own lives with deep wisdom and compassion. The altar holds a glowing electric candle, and the family sometimes also lights a real candle or even a butter lamp (a wick floating in liquified butter). On the altar in front of the statues are seven bowls. Usually the bowls are filled with water. From time to time, the family fills the bowls with incense, butter, flowers, and other offerings. They make the of-

ferings to develop the virtue of generosity. Buddhists believe that happiness in life comes through practicing virtue.

The Tsewangs celebrate Losar, or the Tibetan New Year. Because Tibetans follow a lunar (moon-based) calendar, their new year generally falls in February or March. Tibetans celebrate Losar with a week of ritual dances and other elaborate festivities. To mark the occasion, the Tsewangs bake big, decorative cookies called *bung-gue am chok* (donkey ears) and place them on their altar. They also go to a small Buddhist temple in Columbus to make offerings and to give thanks. Then they toss some barley flour in the air to wish one another prosperity in the coming year.

One year the Tsewangs strung a Losar banner over the doorway of their apartment. In Tibetan script, the banner read *Tashi Dalay,* which means "Greetings." The apartment manager told them to take down the banner. He explained that it was a policy of the apartment complex. But the family had seen other doorways in their building decorated for Easter, Halloween, and Christmas.

Tibetan Buddhism teaches people not to be preoccupied with self-centered thoughts and interests. Tibetan children are taught to calm their emotions. They understand that anger and aggression can be destructive. So the family took down the banner and said nothing

(Facing page) *Images of the Buddha and of Buddhist gods, as well as pictures of the Dalai Lama, are enshrined in the Tsewang family altar.* (Above) *To celebrate Losar, the Tibetan New Year, the Tsewangs make cookies that will be placed on their altar.*

more. But the incident hurt their feelings. "Losar is our holiday," says Tenzin.

Helping others to learn more about Tibetan culture is important to the Tsewangs. They prepare food and give cultural talks at schools throughout the city. They also participate in various local and regional cultural festivals. The most important is the city's annual International Festival, which is held in a large memorial hall every fall. The flyers promoting the Tibetan booth show an image of two snow lions—the mythical guardian animals of Tibet. Under the lions is the word "Peace." The small menu on the flyer offers *shabale* (bread stuffed with meat), *kap-se* (Tibetan cookies), and *cha* (Tibetan-style sweet tea).

Jampa runs a food booth at the festival. "We don't make much profit. Some people sample. Some people don't have money. We give them food." Jampa is clear on one point. "Our aim is to share our culture. We don't talk about politics."

The highlight of the International Festival is a parade across the main stage. All the people who run booths participate in the parade, and thousands of spectators watch. The first few years, Tenzin and Passang joined Jampa onstage in native Tibetan costume. But last year, the children decided not to join their mother. Jampa's friends told her that it was understandable, that her children were becoming teenagers.

One of the ways that the Tsewangs share their culture is by making traditional Tibetan foods.

At the last minute, a Tibetan woman from Nepal appeared at the family's booth. Jampa quickly handed the woman some Tibetan clothes, and the two women represented Tibet in the parade. "I was so happy to have someone to go on the stage with me!" says Jampa.

Tenzin and Passang appreciate their parents' efforts to teach them and other people about Tibet. The children return the attention with hard work and love. Tenzin pays special attention to her father, whom she calls Pala ("Father" in Tibetan). "My daughter does not

(Left) *Tenzin appreciates her father's efforts to help her understand her Tibetan heritage.* (Above) *Jampa addresses a gathering at the International Festival in Columbus as part of the family's commitment to provide information about their homeland.*

like me to drink beer," Tsewang points out. Tenzin explains, "It's not good for him." Tsewang laughs. "I accept that. Good words about my health."

The family often prays together, which helped Jampa after she learned her father had died in India.

 As Tenzin grows older, she is becoming more interested and more aware of her family's history. One day she asked her father for more information, since her Uncle Lobsang is the only member of Tsewang's family she has ever met. So Tsewang told Tenzin the detailed story of his family in Tibet under Chinese occupation. Father and daughter cried together that evening.

Despite the distance, the Tsewangs remain closely connected to their relatives in India and in Tibet. In 1992 Jampa's father died in his sleep at his home in India. Relatives sent word to the Tsewangs in Ohio. When Jampa came home from work, Tsewang gave her the bad news.

"It was really sad. There was nothing much to do but make offerings to the altar and say some prayers. My heart was filled with emptiness being away from my family and missing my father so much that no one could ever know," Jampa says. She applied for an emergency visa and rushed to India to share her sorrow with her family.

On a 1993 trip to Tibet, Tsewang and Jampa spent time with Tsewang's mother, who died three years later.

In the summer of 1993, Tsewang and Jampa went together to Tibet. It was Jampa's first return to her homeland since fleeing as a child with her family in 1959. While they were gone, Passang stayed with Uncle Lobsang in Columbus. Tenzin stayed with a Tibetan family friend in New York City. Neither child objected to the arrangements.

LIFE CYCLES

Tibetan Buddhists believe that life is an ongoing process of development toward achieving spiritual enlightenment. People die and are reborn as they continue their journey toward enlightenment. After Jampa's father's death, a lama told the family that Jampa's father has been reborn as the son of Yangchen, Jampa's youngest sister, who lives in Switzerland. When Yangchen was pregnant, she dreamed of her father. Her mother had similar significant dreams.

Tenzin (second from left) *was able to get to know her grandmother, Jampa's mother, and several cousins during a visit to Switzerland in 1995.*

Tenzin had a good time in New York. "I went there to study Tibetan art. The friend I stayed with paints Tibetan flowers for temples," she says. Tenzin was also able to attend some religious teachings offered by a Tibetan *rinpoche* (religious scholar) living in New York. The scholar has three young daughters, one of whom is Tenzin's age. "I read Tibetan religious texts with them for a month," she explains proudly. Tsewang was happy with Tenzin's progress when she returned to Ohio. "Those people took very good care of my daughter. And she mixed well with them."

Before 1995 Tenzin had met very few of her parents' relatives. That year she and her mother went to Switzerland to visit Jampa's mother, who had traveled there from India. Tenzin also visited her aunts (Jampa's sisters) and cousins.

It was a special trip for Tenzin. "I was very happy when I saw my grandmother. I tried to spend as much time as I could with her. She taught me prayers every day. She always had her prayer book with her. When the children would be doing something, she would sit on a rock and read. I remember one day we went on a hike in the mountains. My grandmother said that it brought back memories of Tibet."

Tenzin was impressed with Switzerland. "They don't litter and they don't participate in wars," she comments.

One day in May 1996, Jampa and the children went to a birthday party for a friend. Tsewang didn't go. He told his family he needed to stay home alone and pray. He says, "A week later, I received a phone call from Tibet [saying] that my mother had passed away. That day, the whole night, I prayed."

Tsewang hoped to obtain permission to travel home to Tibet. He wanted to get there within 49 days of his mother's death to join his family in paying their last respects. (Tibetan Buddhists believe that the process of rebirth begins 49 days after death. During this 49-day period, friends and relative pay their final respects and pray that the rebirth goes well.) But Tsewang's official papers were being processed for U.S. citizenship at the time, so he wasn't able to go.

Instead the Tsewangs sat together in front of their altar and prayed for Tsewang's mother. The family also made small offerings at the altar using a beautiful silver and wood bowl that once belonged to Tsewang's parents. The family put out some tea in the morning, some fruit cookies during the day, and a little drink in the evening—Tsewang's mother's favorite treats. The family continued the special prayers and the offerings throughout the 49-day period.

In 1996 both Tsewang and Jampa became citizens of the United States of America. Tsewang and Jampa proudly display their official certificates of citizenship on the family altar, along with the American flag. Tsewang announces that he is "a little bit proud inside." He adds, "There were people from everywhere [at the swearing-in ceremony], from India, Bangladesh, China, Thailand, Canada, Russia, everywhere."

Each member of the Tsewang family tries to live every day in keeping with Buddhist teachings. They

Family and friends celebrated with Tsewang in 1996 after he gained U.S. citizenship. Jampa earned citizenship a few months later.

An excellent student, Tenzin has set high goals for herself.

try to practice a well-known saying by Tsong Khapa, a famous Tibetan teacher who lived in the 1400s.

This life you must know as the tiny splash of a raindrop,
A thing of beauty that disappears even as it comes into being.
Therefore, set your goal.
Make use of every day and night to achieve it.

(From *Tibetan Folk Tales* by Fredrick and Audrey Hyde-Chambers. Boulder, CO: Shambhala, 1981.)

Meanwhile, Tenzin has been telling her parents for years that she intends to go to Tibet one day. She just may.

FURTHER READING

Dalai, Lama XIV. *Freedom in Exile: An Autobiography of the Dalai Lama.* New York: HarperCollins, 1990.

Heinrichs, Ann. *Tibet.* New York: Children's Press, 1996.

Hyde-Chambers, Fredrick and Audrey. *Tibetan Folk Tales.* Boulder, CO: Shambhala, 1981.

Levy, Patricia. *Tibet.* New York: Marshall Cavendish, 1996.

Pandell, Karen, with Barry Bryant. *Learning from the Dalai Lama: Secrets of the Wheel of Time.* New York: Dutton Children's Books, 1995.

Penney, Sue. *Buddhism.* Austin, TX: Raintree Steck-Vaughn, 1997.

Stewart, Whitney. *The 14th Dalai Lama: Spiritual Leader of Tibet.* Minneapolis: Lerner Publications Company, 1996.

PRONUNCIATION GUIDE

Chemi (cheh-MEE)
Dalai Lama (DAH-lay LAH-muh)
Jampa (JAHM-pah)
Kapchu-la (KAHP-choo-lah)
Kathmandu (kat-man-DOO)
Lhasa (LAH-suh)
Lobsang (LAHB-sahng)
Mussoorie (muh-SOO-ree)
Passang (pah-SAHNG)
Tenzin (TEHN-zihn)
Tsewang (seh-WAHNG)

Tibetan Words and Phrases
bung-gue am chok (boong-GOO AHM CHAWK)
dha-nyen (DAH-nyehn)
kap-se (KAHP-seh)
kata (KAH-tuh)
kenpo (KEHN-poh)
Losar (LOH-sahr)
pala (PAH-lah)
rinpoche (RIHN-poh-shay)
shabale (shah-BAH-lay)
shambu (shahm-BOO)
tashi dalay (TAH-shee dah-LAY)
thangka (TAHNG-kah)
tung-wa (TOONG-wuh)

INDEX

ABOUT THE AUTHOR

Stephen Chicoine was born and raised in Decatur, Illinois. A graduate of the University of Illinois and of Stanford University, he has traveled extensively throughout the world. Mr. Chicoine has written *Journey Between Two Worlds: A Liberian Family* and *Spain* and has coauthored a book for young adults about Lithuania. He is currently at work on several other books for children and young adults. Mr. Chicoine makes his home in Houston, Texas, with his wife and family.

PHOTO ACKNOWLEDGMENTS

Cover photographs by © Brian Vikander (left) and © Stephen Chicoine (right). All inside photos © Stephen Chicoine except for the following: © Brian Vikander, pp. 6, 11 (right), 17, 19; Archive Photos/Adrian Bradshaw, p. 7 (right); Reuters/Corbis-Bettmann, p. 9; © Michele Burgess, p. 11 (left); Robert Calmus, p. 12; Laura Westlund, pp. 13, 34; Corbis-Bettmann, pp. 15, 16 (left), 25; Underwood & Underwood/Corbis-Bettmann, p. 16 (right); UPI/Corbis-Bettmann, pp. 18, 24; Archive Photos/Popperfoto, p. 20; Archive Photos, p. 21; Paul Zanowiak, p. 22; Tsewang family, pp. 26 (top and bottom), 28, 29, 30, 31 (top), 32, 33, 47 (top), 49, 50, 52; James Blank/Root Resources, p. 35. Tibetan rug cut-ins © Stephen Chicoine.